WITH MY EYES
WIDE OPEN

WITH MY EYES WIDE OPEN

MICHAEL FRASER

EXILE editions

singular fiction, poetry, nonfiction, translation, drama, and graphic books

Library and Archives Canada Cataloguing in Publication

Title: With my eyes wide open / Michael Fraser.
Names: Fraser, Michael, 1969- author.
Description: Poems.
Identifiers: Canadiana (print) 20230156320 | Canadiana (ebook) 20230156347 |
  ISBN 9781990773068 (softcover) | ISBN 9781990773075 (EPUB) |
  ISBN 9781990773099 (PDF) | ISBN 9781990773082 (Kindle)
Classification: LCC PS8561.R2978 W58 2023 | DDC C811/.6—dc23

Book designed by Michael Callaghan
Typeset in Granjon font at Moons of Jupiter Studios
Cover/title page image by crngzysrn/Shutterstock
This manuscript was completed with the guidance of A.F. Moritz, as part of
  The Excelsis Group's Mentoring Program, in partnership with BMO Financial Group

Published by Exile Editions Ltd ~ www.ExileEditions.com
  144483 Southgate Road 14, Holstein, Ontario, N0G 2A0
Printed and Bound in Canada by Gauvin

We gratefully acknowledge the Government of Canada and Ontario Creates for
  their financial support toward our publishing activities.

Canada ONTARIO CREATES

Canadian sales representation: The Canadian Manda Group, 664 Annette Street,
Toronto ON M6S 2C8 www.mandagroup.com 416 516 0911

North American and international distribution, and U.S. sales:
Independent Publishers Group, 814 North Franklin Street,
Chicago IL 60610 www.ipgbook.com toll free: 1 800 888 4741

for Anne Fraser

Every Face As a Long Story Short

Waves of Wind Rolling Through Your Hair

Evening Speaks Its Own Language

I didn't know the cost

of entering a song—was to lose
      your way back.

So I entered. So I lost.
      I lost it all with my eyes

wide open.

—OCEAN VUONG
from "Threshold"

EVERY FACE IS
A LONG STORY SHORT

IN PASSING

I felt my father's abrupt kick
storm through the womb's
membrane, its aftershock
surfing years, a shadow even
night couldn't shake.
Who knew my near-death
experience would arise
months before I was born.
My mom didn't know if I
was still me, or the past
tense of me.

Sitting in Ms. O'Brian's
grade two class, we practiced
being quiet, but were captured
by our chests' bicameral pumps
speaking louder than sundog
prairie horizons. Our voices
cocooned within us. We were all
geniuses then, unaware of the
floating life metaphors we freed
from the teeth of spent dandelions.
Those childhood days rest
covered in cloud duvets,
how the branching sky became
another word for forever,
and jockeys rode four seasons
back to their stables.

At fourteen, I sat on our
kitchen floor with a serrated
steak knife's blade aimed at
my near-grown belly.
I envisioned my demise
and climbed down from
the ladder my thoughts
had erected. I didn't know
the sound of rain was the
world exhaling.

DOG DAYS

In 1977 my young jive-talking father
controlled a long white thunderbird
through Toronto's melting July streets,
he parted his badass sideburns and boogied
out our dawn door in bursting colour
a sharp all-spice scent trailing behind him.

A polyester epidemic flooded
the days like a vibrant quilt
my mother forcing tight scratchy clothes
onto my brown twig-like frame
how she was ten women in one
the sleepless breadwinner with an iron heart
and the wounded dawn
searching for a life she could never have.

I remember drunken rum sounds
my father skipping dishes along waves of tiled floor
how he played shaft and superfly
on my mother's tamarind face
blasting her eyes red like a desert wind
then the silent wall of tears behind my closed bedroom door
I remember maple trees were puffed-out afros
in the darkening bowl of night sky.

MS. AGNES

Splayed smile lines jigsawed over
the back of her hands like puzzle pieces,
like two patterned dew-filled leaves,
peaceful as day breezed in.
Those fingers dreamed their way through
tendril nests. It was the early '70s and
we all had "bad" hair in those days.
I can still smell the hot comb raked
through mangroves, as bottles of blue
Cleopatra grease nodded from salon shelves.
Grenada greened like Eden, hugging its
calypso sun. She parceled my world, letting
the world's crooked crack away. I called
her "mom", and she sprinkled love wherever
I stepped. The country girl working as a domestic
in Toronto was abstract to me then, a Madonna
jumping past my head... Today,
I imagine Ms. Agnes petaling from the
layered shadow, and we share tea over a
cork table. What sits at the tale's end, I ask.
You're wet with words, she says. What I
know circles the swiftness of sound. You can
believe in air, or harvest the murmur inside
you. I see her clouded cataracts watch
candlelight flicker the walls' meridians.

DAYDREAMING SOFIA

"I loved them as poets love the poetry
that kills them, as drowned sailors love the sea."
—DEREK WALCOTT

I'm usually superfly, but today I've been flying sick,
down in the corporeal dumps, wounded by green bacterial
waves of chance and happenstance, and saying damn,
what is Sofia doing today while I'm holed up at home
stuck in front of my bambam computer surfing cyberspace
like some lost black Captain Kirk, saying hey now, all the
while thinking of Sofia stuck out in the Venus Flytrap of
wondering, daydreaming of which warm mango countries
she might run off to like a lightening quick gazelle,
sailing moving grooving under a hot burning piping hot
steaming polenta sun, and I'm saying to myself damn that
hip-to-jive Sofia is always moving, always kinetic,
even in her mind she's all go go go, and I want to go with her,
explore the fine confines of terra firma before I burn out fast
like a light bulb exploding into nothing, and I'm thinking
damn that Sofia, I could fall in love with her in two weeks on
vacation, definitely beside a warm beach watching the ocean
waves march in like a foam army of blue green ants,
and I'm thinking damn what is Sofia thinking right now?
and I'm thinking Sofia is fly like a soft rolling fiji wave
coming into the sands of my hello eyes, yes, and I say
damn Sofia is a wave, all curves and showing God's best
work when he was out of his blue period, and there she is
rolling down that piping ribbon of stone highway moving beyond

tomorrow's sepia sunset, into desert lands and badlands filled
with deadheads and nude middle-aged men going through midlif
crises more heartbreaking than a malnourished child on vision tv,
walking through nudist camps like neon Adam and Eve, she's
singing beaming arias and wondering about the old shoe store
neighbourhood back in dead Toronto, which is permafrost to her no
because she's burning up a mile a minute cruising hard into
Mexico, having short women lash out at her in Spanish
because she looks like a rose-coloured Flamenco dancer,
her hair roasting like curled spaghettini in the beat-up Mexican
heat, and crowds of men watching each bounce of her flower
petal ass, standing sitting watching, selling tickets to see the new
hot spiraling babe in town, eyes barreling down her skirt like
lost children, salivating in the psychic wind as it lifts her skirt
and knocks them stone dead with appreciation, and I'm saying
damn that Sofia is everything and anything anyone would ever
want to have, and I'm saying damn I wish Sofia and I could trip
down to Mexico, mingling with the lost descendants of Aztecs
and Toltecs, climbing sun and moon temples like urban
astronauts and saying pow pow pow to low silver shooting
stars when we reach the top, only to fly back down on a winding
beam of worm tequila, vomiting 100 miles/hr in sweet nectar
filled jungles, making love under cricket nights and cactus days,
and I'm saying damn this is all a pipe dream coming out at me
from nowhere, I'm bogged down in permafrost traffic gridlock
neon bike town, and she's out there moving moving moving.

MINDFULNESS

Look at this day
we've stepped into,
a room so vast we can
only attempt to cross it.
Gone is the night chamber
we've abandoned, even
the land's face we've
flown over and left
bathes in a different time,
licks the sea's hem,
whose waves flickered
like a wounded candle
when we looked down
on them. Each person
we pass is also a tourist,
as in we are all day-trippers,
drifters of coincidence,
like buckets of morning
pollen released, each trifling
grain to find its sketched mate
before the last hours turn in,
all the ancient wayfarers now
crumbled like dry leaves,
their names parentheses on the
stone's frown. Pere Lachaise
cemetery is a dewdrop inside
a droplet perched on a nameless
pebble banding a boilerplate star,

and the gleam between us is
all that matters, together,
in this brittle breathing moment,
we are a language no one else
can touch. The air is a type
of door when we feel it.

PERSONALS

after C.D. Wright

Some days I play soccer in my suit,
insinuating myself into pick-up games
fresh from work. I prefer the furnaced heat
of summer. I hate Wednesdays. I've spent half
my life looking for the perfect poem. I love a
bird who makes her nest in Mississauga. I thought
I found the one, but thorns survived the snow. She left.
I have many regrets. I once owned a pet iguana.
He died in a fire in 1993. I lost everything,
but found myself. It's cliché, but true.
I discovered photograph ashes make me cry.
I spend my time walking through biographies.
Time scented on paper. I see my life as a movie.
Chris Rock could play my part. My favourite colours
are chocolate brown and sky blue. These days,
I wear what fits. I need to lose two bowling balls
to be at my high-school weight. The high point
of my life was jumping out of an airplane. What
I loved most was the green silence. They now
say the universe will expand forever.
Everything moving away from everything else.
I can explain later. If you'd like to meet.

PORT CREDIT

The yacht-blue lake breeze
walks beside us, its voice edging
the face of beaming cars,
there's so much light, your waving,
blush-red hair, is a poem
of global importance.

Our flow centers the language
of handholds, together we're
an entire world folded in dialogue,
how we talk the hourglass out of
existence, the way our words braid
into each other, night's reflection a
symphony in your eyes. I didn't know
the zing in your lips was October
holding its song in place.

FIRST

I was five
when it happened.
The Litebrite commercial
fanned across the living room
raking paper-clothed walls
with sound.

Then   like a newborn
catching sunlight,
I saw it.
My finger tips
blinked against the window,
opened up to the chanting cold
like a released bowstring.

My eyes dished round,
back-counting
bushels of flakes.

EDMONTON, 1981

In grade six, our class aced
the school fundraiser. We were
dead last until dad bumbled
in with a month of empties.
It was the '80s and no one narked
when kids off-loaded the van.

The mountain of two-fours
reclaimed our apartment patio.
After school, I scooped up beer bottles
parked around the living room,
sometimes scouring vomit before
mom's keys unfastened the front door.

There were three of us black
in St. Hilda's. My little brother was
the other male. We were the only
ones sporting fros. When Jason
was born, a man called my dad
nigger outside the waiting room.
Security removed him,
but the word refused to leave.

My dad's fists had a thing
for my mother's face.
When they were younger,
he picked her like a lock,
moved into her mind and never left.

On the rotary dial phone,
Ajike told me I was too dark.
Brooke Shields was on
TV hawking her Calvins.

SIDE EYE

Almond-shaped, upturned,
or creasing the brow bone,
it told me seconds after I touched down
that I didn't belong here. I was five
and too young to know it already had
my number, and erased my founders
from any book they tried to squeeze into.
Side eye knew I hated myself before I did,
and stared me down transit aisles, where
I learned to accept its side glance kick,
take ownership for the crime of being.
Side eye salted away my foundation
like stone-slashing water,
left fathomless furrows down my
backbone breadth.
It kept value outside of me.
How I wanted to disappear into exteriors,
have eyes that mirrored sapphire seas,
the joy of another's hair,
coast anywhere without suspicion
and let the sun toast me.

N-WORD

It did more than shatter bones,
on Edmonton's thin-grass soccer fields,
or waiting in bus shelters
with my light tamarind-skinned mom.
These six letters became a caste I could
not shake. At confession I expected
more from Father Kunyk who said
all I had to be was myself.
It is never enough.
Even at her elbow-high age I know
what my daughter feels as she scrapes
its spittle from her hair. When I sense
the deluge framing her eyes, I lie and say
with time it will wither away,
knowing it'll just sink underground,
fangs primed, ready to strike,
and slither out somewhere else.

A DEPORTEE RETURNS

He forgot snow,
the mythical beauty
like cold light beads
tingling through his coat.

He forgot hunger
and how the refrigerator held
three chocolate bars
placed on the middle rack,
drawing eyes away
from the stadium of empty space.

He tried to forget
the constant calling-card
ringing in his mind
the two fatherless children
half-clothed in Grenada.

He tried to forget saying yes
to the neighbour's boy
whose eyes widened
when he parted the fridge.

SOLSTICE

It's amazing how tight the city wears summer.
In the '70s, we tried to stay out till
streetlights began to hum.
Even now, I can hear my father's drunk
laugh cutting through barbecues,
feel the belt-lash sun smacking my pecan skin.
I can't tell you about sunburns,
that's not how I wrinkle.
I can't go to the gym or run outside
when asphalt chars beneath me.
This heat makes buildings grow
palm fronds from their footings.
Even inside, I sweat like a bad lie.
Varieties of red populate 1:00 a.m. fast food spots,
and my stomach's metabolism
responds angrily without me.
The road home strolls through
moon shadow galleries. Deep down,
I think everyone's scared of the dark.
It's what we all fade into.
This city coughs up streets in intervals.
Snooping steep over my shoulder,
night begins the year's daylight decline.

HOG TOWN

Around you there is always Toronto and its
type of sleep where entire lives lather, where
someone is always on the other side of language,
Toronto where neon tweezes night of its stars,
where the sky is on the tip of collapse, Toronto with
its car cigars, the pillaging exhaust insinuating itself into
downbeat air, Toronto that catches itself sweating into basins,
the capital T tapping its lake-reflection like a smoker's hand
dabbing ashtrays, Toronto with its asphalt ring gyrating
and rotating round houses, long intersection faces with
red, green, and amber eyes, Toronto spilling its jokes onstage
during open mic night, how it calls out in steel tongues and
condo glass voices reflecting the afternoon's sun furnace-glow,
Toronto with too many excuses, how University Ave. slips
with bakers' dozens watching a fountain lose and regain
its fear, their mouths slimming grammar to its core,
Toronto beams along its wave-bitten shoreline,
buns its hair, caps its easel teeth, strut-walks its map
of maple blues and winter grey chimney hands, dragging
clouds across the sky's lit incinerator face, like soccer flags
laughing hard out car windows when the World Cup hugs
fiddlehead whistles waving through gathered morning bars,
like a demanding lover, Toronto plays hard-to-get and flies
swallow-fast whenever it picks up the chase, it is cast
iron big-league and always on the cusp of making the playoffs,
Toronto spews its crystal-filled mother's milk feeding children
crowded on splash pads sidestepping day's humid kiln blast,
it swims an arced dogleg home through sunflower-yellow,

mulch-veiled gardens, crossing constantly-renewed corridors,
Toronto swings out car-clogged arteries, past its streetlight
arm hairs, out to the paved fringes of the bee colony collapse,
Toronto sees its working-class shadow first in day's bare
nursling glint, and empties its full dugout bladder adding
debris to runnelling rills in ravine valley river veins,
Toronto with its one charcoal black road, an asphalt ring
like children joining hands round blocks. It sears
its crackling voice on cell phones when every
dumped beta simp didn't know his Juliet's feelings were
tragically unlike the play and temporary, Toronto which
once took down the moon and presented it as a prompt
present of its unbreakable love while evening's sable
horses galloped in, Toronto inhaling the smoke of tenants'
thoughts, a bubbling cartoon largesse as the dusted dusk
skyline and traffic-pitched air continues rigging framed,
hue-soaked canvases for residents to sidle into,
this is the only portrait the concrete heat-island
wants you to fumble during Queen Street's endless
hipster festival, Toronto with its parked car lights
like red nail holes footing lakeside parks, with its
never off-the-rack morning glow, its alloy metallic-blue
glazed lake, its checkered past, its rebar granite
blind insistence, its club-hopping finger scrawl,
its moving heyday, its grafted tongues, its calypso
steel pan notes, its GQ jump-link suits, its burrowing
grotto train tracks, how its happy hour lies nuzzle
ceaseless skies into place.

PAST TENSE

Long before still images gathered into reels,
faked and raked movement across canvas screens,
before our minds grew magnetic, and we unfurled
how the unseen tether held Earth to its satellite,
and polished silver appliances skated from
open-mouthed factories, and oven-baked bricks
mirrored unshaven bi-pedal ambition,
our cave-dwelling stencil footprint grazed along
wildfire-lit walls, grew into centuries blossomed
with hieroglyphs where meru log boats and reed
ships oiled with bronzed-back oarsmen plied
aged seas in half, reaching Tyre and other
hoary-named lapsed lands flung to the known-world's
ends, and returned soaking with Nile sun, cattle,
wares, and slaves. Long before we chipped sandstone
for spearheads on this winged orb where there is a
place on the page for everyone to create their own hue,
our hands reached where stone sparked
the ground's thermal layers, and lumps
of pyrite ignited bullets through wheellock
pistols and the brass brazzle luster of cocked guns
sang with firecracker staccato, and well before
the butcher's stick knife turned pig to ham
and we dried crystalline stinging sea salt to preserve,
pickle, cure, and smoke-hang animal flesh, before
the anthology of constellations and running down
savannah prey, there was a terrene syllable which
grabbed the first carved domino, and firmed it in place.

ODE TO NERUDA

Poetry arrives on this page
calls my name and vanishes
poetry hides in alleys
feeble mouse stalking midnight cats
it wails in the rising sun's ears
and is shattered like dropped clay
voice of fire blaring out radios
a tree shaken without wind
it is an undressed emergency
the death knife in slain abdomens
concrete stained with sonnets.

Poetry is a rumour whose time has come
it break-beats through boom boxes
an unknown quantity on night's skin
poetry races against colours
and carries tomahawks to cast spells
a wounded word crawling at day's end
poetry is a fact that cannot be checked
a windowless event marching south.

Poetry fuels an arms race of lovers
tongues hands lips breasts buttocks
it glides through every neckline
unleashing waves and tremors
your skin a borrowed landscape
poetry flies out your mouth
and makes its nest in your eyes
pupils dilate surrounded by green
poetry touches me with warm hands.

WHEN I BEGAN TO WRITE
after Tomasz Rozycki

When I began to write,
I didn't know my sweat
would turn everything around
me to stone. I didn't know
the sky would rain blood,
my lower-case cuts would
remain wealed, welted, unhealed,
and distance would stalk
you and our family to mask
all away from me. Funny how
the prizes I won, the accolades
I wanted, picked like bronze
statuettes falling from groves
of dew plum trees, can't fill a
single cell in me now. When I
began to write, I didn't know
the planets birthed from my head,
and how I bent and coerced time
with megaphones of punctuation,
would slaughter the now,
and render the real world's
sizzling hues a reflected
distraction. I didn't know what
I didn't know, and now the
poems are loose in brumal
woodland larch, hollowing a
tomb, one handful at a time.

PHOTOGRAPHER

Your charcoal-black camera,
or a room once covered in cloth,
like Szymborska's pen igniting graphite

on hewed treated pulp pages, or a
granular word's crest before it rises
out the mouth's moist tray. You keep

the sun angled over Havana, flip through
the lake blue of Bolivia, and show me a
Cambodian monk's untethered day. Think

of all miracles pushing human flight,
the way air fits round a wing. Your eyes
brushing earth from up there. Reflected

on silver, I said I like your self-portraits best.
You bring light in from outside. Watching you
walk, there's always something I forget to

say. Your latest shot unhooks another grail:
the subway train's aura trails as it spills past
the platform, a few blurred faces, unaware.

TORONTO SUN

This steel-cold factory drinks ink
by truckloads, frees paper to blush
the polished floor's concrete face.
I juice the graveyard shift Friday,
and if I luck out, Saturday too.
On sweep duty, I swing past
everyone twice, nod to my
supervisor, who we know is
banging the lead temp.
She is married with two kids.
They motel it, hours before
our shift lands.
Every face is a long story short
machined through the blue-collar
hum and haze. Outside on smoke
break, union guys jaw – see if Eddie
can open doors, once you're in,
it's f-ing eh! – I don't mention English
and Geography assignments due Monday.
3:30 a.m. lunch, I lie in the recycle
compactor's hyena jaws, somewhat
knowing life's final rest is one push-
button accident away. I'm sixteen
and learning what existence means.

WAVES OF WIND
ROLLING THROUGH YOUR HAIR

PLAZA DE ESPANA

Seville has made us say "uncle"
and surrender to its midday shade.
We gazed our way through
gardens, wondered under a
banyan tree so vast
we were sure its branches
called the city up from its red
dusted earth.
You're a kissable spiced eyeful
flying over clay plaza tiles,
you slink playfully over
low kneeling bridges,
the shallow water beneath
like a steamed moat
made hotter by you
passing over its shores.
The palace calls us in,
what were shadows now
emerge from their ancient shells.
The breeze is a wind instrument,
dreams and inscribes history,
cools the sweat glistening
our skin, tops the season
thriving around us.

ALGARVE

I remember wind racing over
Meia Praia pelting sand grains
straight across low shifted dunes,
how we turned our meager
red-striped beach umbrella to stonewall
the wind's coarse invisible hand.
The sun played hopscotch, draping its
corona bracelet on your supple arms, as
it feathered your legs and fair face,
passing wherever light wanted to enter.
Nights we strolled cobbled paths, our
hands entwined, tethered to the soft-shuffle
rhythm our feet mirrored. The walled
old city handed us centuries of revealed
secrets pouring out candle-lit churches,
restaurants, museums, and palm-lined
gathering squares. We walked uphill
towards the clifftop lighthouse,
silent as a day turning over. We stood
and watched sweeping headlands rise
like stone statues from the ice-bitten sea.
Arms interlaced, our lips touched,
ocean-lit by the setting sun's glowing
seams, and at that precise moment,
I knew the world had no end.

JARDINES DEL ALCAZAR

We are embraced by this
hold of Mediterranean palms
whose frayed, plunging frond leaves
speak breeze-brushed sentences.
Our shoes sun-glitter, momentarily
married to the art-path, glazed tiles.

The banyan tree glimmers and
insinuates its arms and legs along
the ground, establishes itself in
air. We are off-balanced, awed by
how it leans into space. We see
the snail vine and tapeworm plant
are aptly named. The maidenhair
fern spins before us, and still,
for me, your wind-turned waved
curls is the main obsession.

The garden is a clover-green tide
stuffed to bursting: Chinese lantern,
bead tree, manna ash, umbrella papyrus,
pampas grass, itch tree, wintersweet,
silk floss tree, trumpet creeper, lace fern,
soap aloe, century plant, and common
hollyhock. Your eyes reflect this green
feast, and I know I've already eaten
from the good luck plant.

ECHO

You are Spain with
your Miro hands where
paintings spring wet,
and you gain strength washing
time's feet and eating each
remaining petal after your
steps have passed.
You are the throne of
France, narrating lady liberty's
life in wide-mouthed wine
glasses filled with the colour
red. You become Portugal
every time someone on the
planet says Porto and we're
back atop that bus crossing
the heavy metal Dom Luis
bridge, watching the face
of each young Icarus
diving hands-first into long
sardine-scale reflected waters.
You are Belgium, where
newlyweds feed us cake,
setting a Bruges' square
afire with thirsty smiles.
You are Holland with its
tulip army licking landscapes
in vibrant hues, light prisms
spilling colour across

panoramas. If the moment
is a village, I know your
eyes are of global importance,
a moveable armistice
leaning into each calm
sun-dressed day.

HOTEL UNIVERS

The hotel room beside
ours is a bouquet of screams.

We're convinced her roller-
coaster ride is continuous as

her eruptions rumble the floor's
hallways and everyone passes

each other and the chamber maids
with plastered smiles, and shifting,

dilated eyes, the constant smirk,
fresh greeting, our minds swinging

with peeled images, rounded pears,
the metallic red of garter belts, a

silk touchline French-kissing flesh, we
wonder the gravity of their appearance,

is she sea-eyed with heart-shaped lips,
is he chiseled and gym-built to deliver

what is best about this world, both
opening all our doors to other shores.

PICTURE

Your photographs, brilliant
and profound tea leaves I read
into your life, or the first explorers
breaching the Bering Strait,
unaware two vast continents
will converge our human story.
Your hair lengthens back
in time. Poppy red, butterscotch
blonde, and burnt sienna wash
over each other, cling fast
in tendrils like my eyes booked
to your hips. An Amazonian
song spreads through speakers.
You fold words into Venezuelan
Spanish, swaddling jungle border
memories a few steps into Brazil.

WALKING HOME

Walking beside you,
I felt the oak trees
breathe September right through me.

You said, "autumn"
and I was chained
to your marzipan smile
& snowlight green eyes,

I wanted to touch
the slabs of wind
rolling through your hair.

WEDDING #1

It looked like a sham
scaffolded with turned eyes
there in city hall's grey concrete maw.
I numbered all guests on my
left hand fingers. The magistrate
mentioned postponing the date amid
hailstorm sneezes and thundering coughs.

But it was January and we had
to get on with the year. The refugee
application had failed, and Toronto winters
were too cold for compassion.

I slid a headshop ring onto her
twig-thin finger. The blushed gold
was too embarrassed to shine.

To this day,
my parents still don't know.

AFTER MIDNIGHT

The buzzed text, a granular light
alphabet assembled in my black blazer
pocket, when clocks inched
past midnight, I read your message
and kilometers away, our minds touched.
Revelers still locked lips under Times
Squares' fallen cherry-red apple.
I thought of you feeding night's larder
into your camera. The morsels I'd
eventually see. My sleep whirred
strides around your curved lines,
the font assembled your maya blue
corona-eyed visage. In one dream
you wore a hand-made lavender
dress. Its supple hem banked your
walking-hymn hips. Waking, I thought
I felt your willow lips petal across my
chest, but it was the sun's noiseless
canary hand climbing through the window.

MEMORY

These photographs play
like river water through hands.

Winter came early that year.
There was no moss on the bark,

and the earth practiced another turn,
words carried shovels,

and went to lie down in mounds.
The cold brumal sleep of bears.

REUNION

I'm ten minutes late, slinking
into a blue plastic side chair,
when the meeting hits auto-cruise.
Others seem like they're listening
as glazed tables and chairs inch closer
to their reflective somnolent heads.
Who knew it would take
three woven years for your
candle to come around.
Now you open like a
summer door. Not the one
Alice fell through, but the
lavender one your voice
allows me to enter when our
intense conversation blurs the
evening deepening around us.

EASTBOUND

Station, train, station,
everything my soul craves
maps red with danger.
Your black skirt has looped
my mind since the pub,
and each white polka dot
signals another reason why
friendship frails to heated murmur.
We speak in gestures,
your silver left-finger band
widens years over mine.
Our thoughts are on speed-dial
words garnish with smiles,
a subtext easily outsourced
to anyone in eyeshot.
A hug waves us on our way.
I negotiate the platform while
you bound east above electric rails.
We've careened into a beehive
world of decisions,
neither knowing what will come next,
the honeyed buzz, or the allergic sting.

PARK

We lip-danced bordering
railed stairs where the street
briefly shelves over trees,
and streetlights softened the maples'
alpenglow. With palms clicked to
your drawn bottom, my thoughts
perched on technique. An inner
voice said steady this moment,
and I was mindful of roadside
grains, hidden raccoons eyeing
us from the blushed dark, and
the twirling ride centered on your
mint tongue. You said you can
sense Earth's sway. Your body
murmured to reaching hands.
I remembered how the moon
gnawed through crumbling
clouds. Immured under lamplight,
we held each other as if the
leaves had stopped falling.

GOING TO CAPE

Speakers loop the Backyardigans
and our daughter is all smiles,
all song. This drive is becoming
an ode to childhood, a junket
to clear the mind of reason.
Mine has been emptied often
in the engine's hum. We are drunkenly
comfortable with each other, but not
electric. Elm-green trees camp in my
peripheral vision, and behind song-soaked
ears, another missed exit. We are mother
and father, and not, well, you know.
There are rings around Boston, places
to call the hour into being. The interstate
is addicted to signs, writes its name
with numbers. I always knew I'd come
to this point eventually. We live by norms,
a call to expectations. Only the beach
is where it wants to be.

SUBJUNCTIVE

A year before, he said her eyes
were mint leaves gathering, yet she
clung to "no." How different would
things be if he had rested truth on tables.
If he was not glued to marriage. If he had
mentioned this earlier. If they hadn't
clicked. If they could've been friends.
If they hadn't spoken of airplanes, flying
through storms over the Pacific, her Pyrenees
dog wearing white, her love of Goya. If he had
left months before. If summer never ended.
If he had read about mindfulness. If there were
no comedy of errors. He walks the rasping
floor and joins his slumbered wife beneath a
floral comforter. If he could live in the
subjunctive, he would.

A PARTIAL HISTORY OF MY STUPIDITY
after Czeslaw Milosz and Edward Hirsh

The self-help books say ignore
facial scar blemishes
amassed before 18.

Since then, the stream I polluted
overflowed its spillway, sprawled
its reclined fingers
eating the river's mouth and
flooding land's loose tongue.

There was the time I married
and no one knew. Vegas isn't
the only place people go to
hide time. We didn't even
know what to call it.

I took in shortcuts only to
learn it's the scenic route
that uncovers its shine.

Forgive me,
saying I'm only human
is just another thing fumbled,
a spill cats won't lick.

DRIFT

"you can't live on, in that way,
in the past, them day is gone."
　　　　　　　　—JOHN LEE HOOKER

I recall when spring was all-that,
and our two-tone handholds gloved down
the creek path, the way tree buds gambled
against snow. The equinox wind ran like
a child without footprints through slanted
brook banks flipping crocus heads and striped
squill. The water kicked and drummed off
the weir and trailed us hiking the ravine.
You leaned in closer, your eyes gathering
nests of red-sided garter snakes writhing,
yoking on chilled stones beneath your feet.
That night, your crimson head nuzzled my
chest with sleep, and even when your breathing
sawed logs, I knew the world could not stall.

Another blues dose thumps steady out speakers,
shakes me back in a wink.
I know silence only matters when
I move through the house alone.
Another hiking pic debuts on Facebook,
Mount Nemo. You grin with others.
If I had only taken you before the virus
hid voices in facemasks.

My mind is a continent rifting apart—glad for
the bliss ripening within you, not for the
shank ache squalling my interior. You move
in checkerbloom and goat's rue, gaining the
hike's lookout, where bees and butterflies mix the
pollen larder on mist flowers' purple tendril tips.
Everything I thought we'd be doing together.
If I could snatch the air, I'd squeeze it dry.

PROFESSEURE

We could be on La Rambla
nestled between the gothic barrio's
old stone maze
rising like cracked shadows
or indigo walls
of a parted dusk sea.

We'd move through words
voices in full symphony over
our magnetic heads, you the soft north
to my hard south,
taking in our world at all points
a table for two at the end of this line.

We'd be good liquored up,
our feet painting the Catalan art scape,
each step equaling Miro's
radiance and measure.

If time had an opposite,
it would be us.
We'd go where the heat is,
following canary sand beads,
your dog Luna a swift universe
leaping at the lead's tail.

EVENING SPEAKS
ITS OWN LANGUAGE

ORACLES OF MARCH

Everyone's life moved inside
past the hand sanitizer
guarding the mudroom.
Sarah's tablet told her the
pound sign's name is "octothorpe."
Her youngest laughed as he
repeatedly tried to pronounce it.
Still, the letters remained stuck to
his teeth. She and the kids decided
to disappear in math.

Beyond closed windows,
streets and sidewalks happened
without them. The shingled roof,
wind-blown, and missing a few
black sand tiles, mirrored the
street's deadline.

It was amazing how the
invisible possessed us.
They said it was nature letting go,
but the weak didn't always ditch first.
Seasons fell outside house windows.

Before, there were more nurses,
then there wasn't.
Schools were open, then they folded.
Once, you could meet hands,
then you couldn't.

LOOKING FOR THE WEATHER LADY

This raving unbroken rain, like misery's
frantic messenger ambling door to door,
pounding to be let in. A Fox News anchor
turns more myth, his voice a spinning wheel

of verbal violence, a pinch of arsenic garnishing
soup. Outside the plant, a man yells, "A suit
stole my bootstraps." The sky blazes like the 4th of July.
If we were American, we'd be drunk dodging

lightning bolts under water-steeped maples,
sparklers crackling above our hands. I'd mention
my job slipped away and you'd laugh from the
rum's mind-shudder. Repelled by this warring

night, the cats abandon the window ledge, snuggle
in valleys between our legs. You crave movies,
but I'm rolling through channels, looking for the
weather lady, wondering how long this will last.

TORNADO WARNING

Those spinning clouds swarm
flat sun-fed skies easy as wolves' teeth
latching deer. Something about rolling
low pressure downdraft flies from screens.
The forecaster runs out of doom
superlatives. Viewers seam to
net images, momentarily forget
to hightail it to the basement hatch.
Rumpled and wound, the air winches,
whipsaws and winds whir like
when rooms waver and swirl
following ledged nights on
the town. Reports touchdown,
two funneling bulls goring
etched landscapes, abrasive
whisks charting their own
slapdash fault lines.
For those huddled
in unfastened paths,
it's the falling hang
glide of moments,
how we've placed
bets on the space
we take, and
what nature
assigns us.

AMBER ALERT

This wavering sky and dust-up
leaf-slinging winds charcoaled as massed
crows chasing Tippi Hedren, or the

clawed rail line whir of cloud bellies
bearded with rain... Amid crawling tail
lights the doctor says a furuncle is a boil,

then authorities clatter in past the radio scratch,
another divorced parent gone bat-shit mad.
You say you remember the last one. The greasy

spoon crowd hinged to a stop, televisions
animate with reporters. It was a father, crumpled
his fortune pulling rigged slots. In time kids

might prune curse words, learn to evade fervent
hinky-voiced adults. Windshield wipers retweet
cleared instants. In this moment strained

through rear-view mirrors, we are becoming
others, with nothing left to salt away. The entire
world wide-eyed for an emerald Ford sedan.

INSURRECTION

For a few hours the planet was
in one place again.
We eyeballed screens
saying "What the…!"
as the banner-filled mob undressed windows
and strolled through slave-cast chambers,
their hats another mark of the least.

The trident word phrase fell from
inmate tongues hauling days in
for-profit prisons. Even guards awaited
the real-time, riot-cop beat down,
but had to sink into their own disbelief.

The words became grown triplets
as news anchors said bad things always
come in threes. There's only so much
reporters can say when language breaks
and bathes screens in riot red.

Dawn opened and widened
it's own lens, everyone
watching a cloud-dotted sky
ask for silence,
how angry people thin
even the largest of spaces,
how a nation gasps for air.

GABI

The world unveils
itself in numbers
so many eyes
watching you trace thoughts
across waiting blackboards
the chalk curling figures
like dancers' skates
on fresh ice.

How the shy children
grabbed your myrtle heart
and grew in the sun
of your words
to cast their own shadows
with branched arms reaching
out across the road
and your soft memory
leading the way.

TEXT

Streetcar, subway, store,
outside's plastic frisbee sun,
and my cell phone's signal
zooms between towers.

I can't tell her what I'd like to say.
My fingers are too large
when I text vertically.

                          Buildings mirror clouds
and I stop the sky above Bay St.
Digital photos weigh scratch.

At least the old black and white
said something. I liked how polaroids
took time to disappear, the way god
did when I aged into questions.

I know I have to untether the past, but
my better judgment still resides in last May.

When she centers my mind, language spills
and scatters.
                 More than anything,
I want the comfort words bring,
splashed across portable screens.
or sailing to my ears.

Waking each dawn is overwhelming.
Morning and afternoon's conference knits
with fog, lengthens the hour's interval.

Waiting is an affliction in a world
built for speed.

TIPPING POINT

I should have skipped the horror matinee,
I'm tired of brothers flashing out first.
Outside, evening speaks its own language.
Yonge St. is a headshop strip mall,
a drifting rat, on sale, cash-grab gauntlet.
Our light-skin preference scours eyes
in storefronts. They know black Barbie
doesn't sell, but even displays crave tokens.
My childhood skids to a stop in a *Good Times*
poster as kissing brown-orange-yellow
oval Apollo wallpaper redials 1974.
Dank basement records fuel hipster
drool with Technicolor.
Nostalgia only dreams of itself.
Still, store owners gather firewood for
the shrine to time. In front of pyramid
displays of Maga hats, passing teens
rewire their brains with screens.
The *Leave It to Beaver* playing cards are
more than a pastime, but a passed time!

LEARNING TO FLY

Was still a child then, weary of bedtime
knowing the bodysnatching nightmare mob
would eventually arrive and outpace me.
I always woke to shaking, thinking all the
demons were salivating under my bed.
Then one night, the leash untethered.
I said I liked the land's skirt and flew
over its quilted belly, escaping the
scratch-faced zombie crowd that pursued me.

In high school my focus morphed and
my heady dreams designed a woman who
hovered and swooned with my words,
the twist of flowers shedding from her hair.
She swirled up and down like a kite, and I
flew to join the joy within her.
Now, I flit and swoosh, mindful of any
dream's urgent demonic turn.

PROM

The teeth-grin Trini tailor
wrapped unlimited jokes
tagging rustic Grenadians
as docile under breadfruit trees
while he ran taped numbers down
my pant length, then apologized
when I unearthed my birthplace.

My date Sarah said I bought
the wrong suit. If there was
a domain for taste, I wasn't in
it. The flowers sufficed, yet she
still shaped the night with
down-turned lips.

Our boat was a bonnet
blue-glazed in Toronto harbour.
We unrolled Grand & Toy admit-one
tickets and drank the owners into
ice-cube-cold debt. Sound of dance
feet bubbling from stern to starboard.
The yacht rocked. We didn't breathe
deep enough to say goodbye
to our youth.

FOREST HILL

Dad and I churned
paint buckets prepping to hue
Dr. Solway's weather-aged walls.

I laddered the roost side
and climbed raked metal steps,
dreadlocks slinking windblown
past my shoulders.

I leashed to the view in a
finger-snap. Swank stone cribs
muraled the corsaged setting,
prize cars flared drawn driveways,
and the postman's face was a
TV playlist blaring the 1950s.

I didn't realize what the mailman
was thinking when he locked eyes
on me and race-horsed down those
pristine lawn-sided streets.

Police flashed-in, plentiful
dusk mosquitoes, as I clasped
the roller, drip-marking concrete.
Dr. Solway's voice smoothed
the fuzzed frayed air.
I looked up at the clouds
shapeshifting as they glided by,
jealous of their freedom
to simply take up space.

WHO'S YOUR FAVOURITE CHARLIE'S ANGEL?

We got the strap for it.
Me and Pablo slackjawed in
St. Hilda's Catholic School.
Farah sublet his locker,
Jaclyn bunked in mine.
Principal Jeri made his cameo
swinging a rawhide strip.
There was no laugh track when
the secretary twisted my arm in place.
My right hand burned for hours
echoing the split-leather heat.

In high school,
you could be the biggest weirdo,
and I'd be nice to you.
I opened that way, like drunks
handshaking New Year's Eve.
If you were pretty, I made you
queen and granted you dominion
over my senses. If you were hot,
I was parched prairie grass,
waiting for you to burn me.

MIDLIFE

after Jennifer Chang

When will I unearth this living?
Peel its shell and taste the hard light
within. At Sunnyside Beach, the moon's
first toe dips naked in rolling water.
My house is a small ode of bricks, a cog
in a collection of rows. I am a collection of cells.
If I were to choose another name, I'd let it flutter
ahead of me and watch it crumble the front door.
The threshold of wanting. Decades before this
present obsession, I could smell rain and hear
the universe breathing. All those monsters stuck
in closets. I want to name something that isn't there,
find meaning in floorboards, know there isn't mold
lurking behind the drywall. I know existence
would be simpler if I was sound. If I was only a phrase.
Unlike matches, I don't begin with fire. I begin.

HUNTERS IN THE SNOW

It's as if this panel frame holds us all.
The men are muted in snow, a meagre fox
bleeds into the leader's jacket as daylight
falls like a trembling crake arrowed from
the numb sky. This is the season death builds.
The innkeeper's daughter, whose hands hide
sunken in her gathered kirtle, eyes steel blue
like the downhill horizon's chilled ponds,
inhales the pig's bristled singed skin,
her stomach wide with its own vacancy.
She knows her father can roast anything,
the dried hay stalks like a magician's trick
spilling from his arms.
The ice, dotted with children,
stages a coup against the months' labours
trudging through a stretched dusk.
Each snow-dusted branch is a church steeple
placed on its side, looking ahead, not up.
This is how faith turns a landscape.

STAGE FOUR

I remember the first time her voice
feathered up my face,
and how the groundswell
furnished my skin.
She was spring's
birthstone, murano glass dressed
with light, the northern spy apple
minus snow, even the lake listened
and mirrored her white stippling shorts.
Her scent walked with me braided through
the house, our cottage hands freeing
sand-weathered doors.
Sometimes she was winter's ice-water falsetto
waving at the solstice. The judge arrived at a
pulled-tooth hour, and she
felt the slack in her life transpire. She said the lump
sat growling under her armpit and my thoughts
drained with the tub. When her pruned hair shrank
to peach fuzz, we grew tighter together with each
shivery word crawling off her faint tongue.
The sickroom marathon she ran failed to offer an
extension. Blotches swelled like wood smoke
beneath her eyes as she felt the chafe and shudder
of the crab's sidewise sty.

TAXI DRIVER

Travis never knew what to say,
awkwardly aware he stood outside
Betsy's language. She arrived in his mind
like a daily circular squeezed through
a closed-door mail slot. Any woman
could instantly freeze a man,
shrink him to jitters, if he favored her.
The porn theatre first date was a bad idea.
Reading the newspaper headline,
she had to admit, she didn't think Travis had
a heroic bone in him. With pushups, his body
wound spool-tight. To think, this cabbie actually
considered rain's meaning, a runaway's lost haiku,
her mother's pain ripening, the carte blanche
of cleared streets, how loneliness fills a day.
Was he alive after the gunroom broil,
or did she imagine another timeline
flickering in his rear-view mirror?

ELEVATOR TO THE GALLOWS

Julien's arm snuck towards sunset
filtering through the stalled elevator's door.
He told her there'd be handholds after work,
once he elbowed her husband away.

She snapped her purse to heartbeats
re-hanging the noir receiver after her
lover's voice faded to a stop.

This is how things unfolded.
Someone said something about murder,
a stolen car, a pistol, and the femme fatale.

Owning the screen, Jeanne Moreau was a
jazz invocation legging down the Champs-Élysées.

The old men had seen it all many times before.
They knew he wasn't coming before she did.
Only a woman in love could walk like that,
one of them chimed. Only a woman in love
could wait hours oblivious to rain.

How could he have known the lift would freeze
between floors. How could he have known that
in movies the bad guy never wins.

TO BE CONTINUED

The sketchiest tiffs grip Toronto:
humbled by two rioting blizzards,
Canadian forces careen downtown drifts
outflanking winter squalls, the school
board boss cribs words, and our crackhead
mayor Ford is a peach connoisseur—*he has*
more than enough to eat at home.
Grabbing microphones, he takes the
sacrament of confession, and never lets go.
We are wed to peripheries. The water cooler
knows who scored last night's rose,
and who bathed in thorns to secure immunity.
It's the peacock parade of parasocial ties.
My friend claims he can wiggle his ears.
I tell him there are better talents.
He says, he knows, just ask the mayor.

RAPTURE

Is there a safe word to escape?
I can't take my local bar anymore.
The fiscal cliff fills drinks during
happy hour. On CNN I saw
republicans returning from space.
I want the Nobel Prize for being.
Prisoners, sinners, and saints will
corral together, covered by the syntax
of a great sentence.
It will rise over hills and buildings like a page,
dog-eared in time. Peter will call
from the landfill, and a press
conference will materialize.
At midnight, we'll hear something
about the Mayan calendar.
Let me tell you about the nostalgia
implanted in our species.
When it finally arrives, we'll all
ask is this really happening,
and a dusted voice will say, yeah,
just keep a hand on your wallet.

ACKNOWLEDGEMENTS

Eternal gratitude to the editors of the publications in which some of these poems have appeared, sometimes in different forms: *ARC, Best Canadian Poetry in English 2013, Contemporary Verse 2, EXILE Quarterly, Existere, Freefall, I Found It at the Movies, Juniper, Poet to Poet: Poems Written to Poets and the Stories that Inspired Them,* and *Prairie Fire.*

Thanks to the following people for their advice, time, love, and support: Jean King, Karri Hutchinson, Al Moritz, Michael Callaghan, Gabriela Campos, Fior Tavares, George Eliott Clarke, Beatriz Hausner, Myna Wallin, Molly Peacock, Alice Burdick, Khadijah Jabari, Krystyna Wesolowska, Diane Bracuk, Barry Callaghan, Rami Al-Khatib, Maria Carnevale, Carol Morrison, Heather Wood, Jim Nason, James Deahl, Ildiko Nagy, Tara Haas, Nathalie Paquet, Raza Ali, Valerie Kaelin, Rosemary Sadlier, Charlene Diehl, Barbara Schott, Suzy Taylor, Phoebe Wang, Pablo Garcia, Fauzya Alarakhia, Afsaneh Ezhari, and Monique Twigg.

Thanks to the Plasticine Poets. The Plasticine Poets are: Charlie Petch, Lisa Young, Kate Flaherty, Lisa Richler, Susie Berg, David Clink, Rod Weatherbie, Mary Rykov, Dave Noel, Robin Richardson, and Phoebe Tsang.

Copious thanks to the Toronto Arts Council, Ontario Arts Council, and the Canada Council for the Arts.

ABOUT THE AUTHOR

Michael Fraser of Toronto was published in *Best Canadian Poetry in English,* 2013 and 2018. He has won numerous awards, including *Freefall Magazine*'s 2014 and 2015 poetry contests, the 2016 CBC Poetry Prize, the 2018 Lampe/Gwendolyn MacEwen Poetry Award, and the League of Canadian Poets' 2022 Lesley Strutt Poetry Prize. To complete the book Michael worked with A.F. Moritz as part of The Excelsis Group's Mentoring Program, in cooperation with BMO Financial. *With My Eyes Wide Open* is his fourth poetry collection.